SELFISH HEALING

VENITA MILLS

Dedication

I dedicate this book to myself, my family, my friends, and a special dedication to my brother Eric Dean, Jane Jordan and Edgar Dassau, and to people all around the world who are struggling with moving forward, who are struggling with knowing that it is okay to not be okay, who are struggling with self-love, self-care, and who are struggling with letting go. This book is for you. I hope it brings you extreme comfort, becomes an eye-opener and an amazing life changer.

Acknowledgement

I would like to express my gratitude to the people who have been a guiding in my life, and during the writing of this book. First and foremost, I want to thank God Almighty for making all things possible. Secondly, I also want to thank my mom Linda Dean who has been very vocal in my life with extensive words of encouragement. I want to thank my cousin Antonio Terrell, for being a source of calmness during life's storms. Thank you to my children Paige, Cierra, Keante', and Jalen Johnson, your unconditional love has been my greatest blessing. I extend my thanks to Amelia Walker for all that you have done for me. Thank you to Bernice Granville, and Jacqueline Sparks, you ladies gave me what I needed, when I needed it. Thank you to all my friends who have supported me with the writing of my book and in my life, I am truly thankful. If I missed anyone, please forgive me. I want to thank you all for being in my life that has shown me support, pushed me, and encouraged me every day. Without you, this book would not have come to life.

TABLE OF CONTENTS

Dedication………………………………………………3

Acknowledgement………………………………………4

About the Author………………………………...8

Chapter 1
Being Poured Into…………………………………9

Chapter 2
Permissions………………………………………10

Chapter 3
GOD Is Not Through…………………………………11

Chapter 4
Being Plugged Into…………………………………12

Chapter 5
A Mustard Seed…………………………………...14

Chapter 6
Feeding My Spirit……………………………......15

Chapter 7
Choosing Peace………………………………...18

Chapter 8
Journey…………………...………………………19

Chapter 9
Jealous Spirit………………………….....……20

Chapter 10
Choosing You………………………………………21

Chapter 11
Being Alone……………………………………………………23

Chapter 12
Trust the Process…………………………………………24

Chapter 13
Closed Doors……………………………………………...26

Chapter 14
Being Broken……………………………………………..28

Chapter 15
He Has His Hands on You………………………………....30

Chapter 16
Crying & Praying…………………………………………31

Chapter 17
Acceptances………………………………………………32

Chapter 18
Not Enough……………………………………………….33

Chapter 19
Love Yourself…………………………………………….35

Chapter 20
Tell Yourself…………………………………..….....37

Chapter 21
Being Alone With GOD…………………………………38

Chapter 22
Releases…………………………………………………39

Chapter 23
Better Version…………………………………………...40

Chapter 24
Forgiving Yourself…………………………………...41

Chapter 25
Restore……………………………………………43

Chapter 26
Choose Self Respect………………………………44

Chapter 27
About You………………………………………...45

Chapter 28
The Real You……………………………………46

Chapter 29
Removals…………………………………………47.

Chapter 30
Points to Remember………………………………...48

Chapter 31
Clarity from GOD………………………………..49

Chapter 32
Eviction…………………………………………..50

Chapter 33
Winning…………………………………………..51

Chapter 34
Healing a Wound…………………………………52

About the Author

Greetings, I am Venita Mills, a 47-year-old residing in Houston, Texas. I proudly embrace the role of a mother to four wonderful children. Originally from Orlando, Florida, I was born to Linda Dean and the late Oscar Johnson. As I embarked on the journey of writing my book, I found myself navigating through dark corridors of depression and battling numerous suicide attempts. Within the pages of my book lies a narrative woven from pain, hurt, and the turbulent experiences of my life. The title holds profound significance, reflecting the depths of my journey. To truly understand me is to delve into the intricate layers of my story, intricately woven within these pages.

Being Poured Into

I cannot always pour into anyone, and they cannot always replace.

It is disheartening when someone must come along and tell you the value of something that was once in your house.

You may have all the money in the world to buy whatever you desire, but have to beg for what you need.

When the tables turn, tell them do not lose your appetite, consume that hurt or anger like I did.

A new **DEVIL** brings a new **DEVIL** that requires a **NEW YOU**.

If everything else is leveling up, make sure you level up as well.

God will never give you something that does not belong to you. **#WALK**

You can't change the way people act; you can only change the way you interact with them.

Engage with people for what they're good for in your life. Everything isn't always everything for everybody, because everybody is not created the same way.

Permissions

Give yourself permission to do what is right for you.

Even if that means disappointing others and their expectations of you.

Choose your peace of mind and protect it, no matter the situation.

Tell yourself that you are confident in your ability to speak your truth, communicate how you really feel, and what's best for you.

Respect the cycles in your life and trust that your season of pure abundance is coming.

God Is Not Through

You are in the process of becoming what GOD wants you to be.

The reason you keep waking up is because GOD is not through with you yet.

He keeps waking you up, because he still has something for you that you have yet to receive, but you must start living your life with expectations!

You must start expecting wonderful things to happen for you and to you for it to happen (manifesting). It's the law of attraction.

The Bible says, **"A man is as he thinketh."** If you live your life in expectations, whatever those expectations are, that's what will happen to you and for you.

You are enough, no matter what.
There is a battle being fought that you don't have to be a part of.

Sometimes you have to shut the door to fear, negativity, doubt, unworthiness, confusion, and people.

Because not everybody around you will be able to handle what God is about to do in your life.

Being Plugged Into

Angels do not live in hell.

You have to create a peaceful environment for yourself.

Foundation is Necessary.

Be careful who you allow to plug into you.

We allow people to plug into us, who were not authorized by the manufacturer. Your wealth, health, and peace of mind are unattainable

You have to be selfish with yourself, your peace, your love, your perseverance.

The only thing you must feel guilty about is loving the wrong person.

People sometimes have to be careful of how they treat the person that GOD sent to heal them.

It can be pain today, but strength tomorrow.

Don't you dare doubt your worth or the beauty of your truth.

Embrace who you are unapologetically, not who people expect or want you to be.

You have to know when people's part in your life story is over, so you won't keep trying to raise the dead.

Nothing just happens without reason. Accept it as the WILL OF GOD! Always have the gift of GOODBYE!!!

A Mustard Seed

Matthew **17:20** said it best, "If you have faith as small as a mustard seed, you can move mountains."

Every day, you remind yourself that you are an overcomer.

You must have faith the size of a mustard seed, because through Christ Jesus all things are possible.

If a grain is all the size of faith you need to move a mountain, that's power.

We spend more time believing in others and believing in the seeing, than the unseen.

Just think about it, if all we need is that grain of faith to move a mountain, how much time and energy do you think that would actually take?

Some of us only believe in things we can see, touch, and smell. But those things are only valuable for a moment

Things that we can't see, touch or smell is priceless.

Feeding My Spirit

Luke **1:37** "For with God nothing shall be impossible. This chapter gives you an insight into me.

I can't say if I am a Christian or even religious.

However, I am a spiritual person. I am a woman of God. I do fall short of the glory of GOD every day.

I am not perfect and do not proclaim that I am.

But I do know who God is, and I am a living human testament of all that he has done for me.

When I was going through my storm of depression, suicide, divorce, emptiness, unworthiness.

I turned on my Bluetooth and started listening to gospel music, in doing so, I was being ministered to.

I was getting ready for work, and I was getting fed in such a way that once I got in my car to drive to work, I continued listening.

I didn't even realize that I began to worship GOD in a way I never had before.

That ride to work was just me and GOD. It does not matter where you are, you can always praise GOD.

No matter what your days or nights are like, your spirit will always allow you to know that nothing is impossible with GOD.

Have you ever praised GOD so much that all you can do
is cry, and say thank you, GOD?

That is me. I was told that even when you can't find the
words to say to GOD, Your tears speak for you. GOD hears
tears too. By the time I get to work, the glory of GOD is
upon me.

I have been through a lot in my life. When I think about
all that I have been through, I realized that GOD was with
me and saw me through or even carried me.

So now when I praise GOD, the tears are of joy,
gratitude, and knowledge of who GOD is in my life.

GOD never promises that there will always be good
days, but he did promise to never leave you nor forsake you.

I realized after I left my spouse for infidelity and GOD
placed me in a place to be alone that I had suffered in
silence for years.

I kept my mouth closed about a lot of things and
feelings and I am sure she did as well.

My marriage ended because she said she didn't want the
responsibilities of a marriage anymore.

She was a very impatient person that was not willing to
wait on anything or anybody to get their feet planted to
become grounded. She always compared either me or our
marriage to others.

I would tell her that every individual is not the same, nor
is every marriage the same. Some people will always tell or

show you the good in the marriage, or what they have accomplished in the marriage, but will not tell you the bad in the marriage.

Those times that they actually gave up on each other, the arguments, the separations, etc... Never look at someone else's life or situation thinking that it is what you desire. Everyone's story is different.

That was one of the most devastating and humiliating times in my life. But when I tell you GOD is awesome, he is awesome. I am no longer angry, hurt, holding on to resentment, hatred, or holding a grudge.

I can admit that I am grateful to her for the lesson that she taught me.

Without her doing what she did I would never have been able to see me for who I really am.

I fell in love with me, I became selfish with me, and I found the true meaning of individual happiness.

Sometimes we look for others to give us the things that we are capable of giving ourselves. Being with someone is supposed to add to what you have already given yourself. Love, happiness, peace, assurance...

I have elevated myself in ways that I never could have imagined in my personal, professional, and spiritual life.

Choosing Peace

Choose peace above all else, for life is too short to be involved in anything that GOD didn't set forth.

You may not be where you want to be in life, but if you think about it, you are not where you were.

Proverbs 18:10 says, "The name of the Lord is a strong tower; the righteous run into it and are safe."

Proverbs 16:24 says, "Pleasant words are a honeycomb, sweet to the soul and health to the bones."

Proverbs 19:8 says, "The one who gets wisdom loves life, the one who cherishes understanding will soon prosper."

Romans 8:18 says, "Consider that our present sufferings are not worth comparing with the glory that will be revealed in you."

I know sometimes there are days when you wish you could change something or everything that happened in your past.

Then you realize that there is a reason the rear-view mirror is small and the windshield is so big, because where you are headed is much more important than what you left behind.

Journey

Your journey is unique, and so is the journey of others. If you meet someone on a certain path, offer them encouragement.

You have overcome wounds that were meant to be fatal, but no weapon formed against you shall prosper.

A weapon may form, but it will not prosper.

Remind yourself every day that this is your winning season.

Philippians **4:13** states, "I can do all things through Christ Jesus who strengthens me."

The devil will never prevail if you stand with GOD. Remember, no battle is yours to fight. "Vengeance is mine," says the Lord.

Jealous Spirit

A jealous spirit will cause people to mistreat those who
were sent to be a blessing.
A person's ego and pride will damage relationships,
friendships, and the individual themselves.

When you do not submit to someone, they get mad when
you do not leave room for their pride.

When this happens, you awaken the relationship demon.

Can you recall a time when the devil came in to disrupt
your peace, and you handled it in a way that surprised you?
Just know that it was GOD who had already prepared you
for it.

He may have revealed it to you in a dream or a persistent
thought, but he did not show you when or how it would
come, or where you would be when it did.

Being in God's peace blocks anger, negativity, and demonic
spirits from affecting you.

God may allow the devil to
Come, but he will not allow him to stay if you serve,
believe, trust, and have faith in him alone.

God is a jealous God, and he will not tolerate you putting
anyone before him. Always choosing God, I promise you
can never go wrong.

Choosing You

Choose harmony; choose to put your mind at peace.
Mute out all the noise about your failures and your
shortcomings.

We all fall short of the glory of God. Instead shout
about your accomplishments, and consistently remind
yourself of the capabilities you possess.

Remind yourself that you have survived all the previous
challenges. Tell yourself if you can survive those things
with God's help, you can handle this too. Repeat to
yourself, **"I AM CAPABLE"**

God places you where he wants you to be. God does not
make mistakes. If he calls you into a position, no matter
how overwhelming it is, it's because he believes that you
are the right person for the job.

Ask God to show you, yourself in his kingdom.
If he has placed you in that position, he sees you there.

Divine Creator, grant me the vision to see myself as you do
in your kingdom. If you have placed me there, let me
perceive myself through your eyes, knowing that your
wisdom guides me to where I belong.

Sometimes our greatest prayer should be for God to
open our eyes so we can see who we are supposed to be.
Trust that you are in this position because no one else could
do it like you, should not compare yourself to others.

The present shapes the future; everything happens for a reason. Events in your life may shift your expectations of the future.

Sometimes it's not always necessarily bad; it's just an eye -opener.

Know that you are on the right path. The change you desire is coming.

Sometimes it may seem like you take 3 steps forward and get pushed 10 steps back.

Keep moving forward because there is light on the other side.

You just have to weather the storm. Later, you will see how you have grown through what you have endured….

Being Alone

It's important to understand that it's okay to be by yourself. Sometimes, being alone is necessary to hear God.

God sometimes places you alone because he wants you to realize that you don't need anybody but only him.

One thing to remember is that **"GOD does everything for a reason"**, if something is happening in your life, because GOD is trying to show you a purpose.

Being in a state of aloneness is not without reason. GOD allows it to happen to show you something important.

The lessons he is trying to teach you will become clearer when you take the time to listen.

Yes, it will be challenging, because we focus too much on being alone or what caused you to be alone. But God is saying you are alone because he needs you to listen better.

Don't let others make decisions for you when God has already made them on your behalf.

Trust the Process

Trust the process. Understand that this whole journey is a process.

All the tears, the late nights when you couldn't sleep, the adversity. They are all part of the process.

People will tell you NO, but that's just a part of the process.

GOD is preparing you for something big and you can't even imagine.

Sometimes we get so caught up in asking why this or why that, that we fail to see what God has in store for us.

But you'll never receive anything if you don't go through the process. You can't deviate from it, you can't take a detour - you have to go through it.

Understand that there will be a struggle in the process, but the beauty lies in the struggle.

It's preparing you, building you up, making you stronger. All you have to do is **"TRUST THE PROCESS"**.

No matter how dark things may seem, no matter what others say about your situation, it's not over for you yet.

You can mess your own life completely up and then turn around and get it all the way together.

Once you know better, you do better.

You are okay, no matter what has happened or what you feel like you have lost.

You can still achieve that degree that you want, that house you desire.

You are okay, you are simply in a process. Your best days are ahead of you, not behind you, so stop reflecting on the past.

Pull yourself together and stop beating yourself up because you are in a process. God is processing you, preparing your blessing. **TRUST THE PROCESS.**

Closed Doors

When someone closes a door in your face, all you have to remember is that when GOD allows them to close that door, all He wants you to do is walk up the hall or the street.

There are more doors you have yet to knock on or enter into street. GOD has a better door that He wants you to go through than the one that was shut in your face. Do you know how powerful you are?

You are powerful when your gift matches GOD's grace. **(WHEW!!)**

Get ready and buckle up because GOD is getting ready to show you and everyone who counted you out, who tried to stop you that they can't block the level of grace that is on your life.

GOD's grace and your gift alone are a dangerous combination.

Your wisdom did not come without pain. Until you follow your dreams and get connected to your gift and to GOD, you will never be truly happy.

You have to chase that dream before you die.

You should go and live that dream, whatever that dream may be.

God puts your real life in your imagination. Your real life is not in your present circumstances, nor is it in your current situation. Your real life is not in your paycheck.

Your real life is tucked away in your imagination.
Albert Einstein said
"Imagination is everything; it's a preview of life's coming attractions".

Once you understand that and stop looking at your imagination as hocus - pocus, it opens up a wide range of possibilities. I would hate it if you die and never do the things that you were born to do. Just think about it for a minute.

That one thing or those things that you've imagined doing are the things that you should be manifesting and doing. Stop allowing fear or other people to discourage you from doing it. Step out in faith, I promise GOD has you.

Being Broken

When you were broken and hurt and did not take the time to heal. You just moved onto the next relationship without realizing that you are very dangerous at this point.

You have to know how to survive alone when things go left, you are to go right. No pressure, no stopping, no test, no testimony, no work, no reward, no fight, no victory.

You are a person who should always build on survival, not excuses. Don't allow someone to tell you they love you or that you were trying to love and then mess over you, and you allow it. You are diminishing your worth as a person.

You don't deserve anyone's disrespect, no matter who they are. You don't deserve anyone's abuse (mentally, emotionally, physically, and verbally). You don't deserve anyone's love that has conditions. If whoever cannot build you up when you are down or add positivity to your life, then that person is not the one for you.

Respect yourself enough to walk away from anything and anyone that no longer serves you, grows you, or makes you happy. If you are not being treated as the Queen/ King you were born as, with love, respect, and honor check your price tag.

Maybe you marked yourself down for that type of treatment. It's you that tells people what your worth is.

Get off the clearance rack and get behind the glass where they keep the valuables. You can no longer exist in someone's presence without it triggering a thousand wounds.

You are either going to dim your light and share a space with them and detriment yourself or not share space at all. You get to choose. Understand that it will always be that way unless they decide to heal and join in on all the happiness on their own.

Surround yourself with people that are genuine, that have your best interest at heart, that actually want to see your light shine brightly. That supports your ups as well as your downs. Life is too short to be misery's company.

He Has His Hands on You

Luke **4:18** says, "The Spirit of the Lord is upon you, because he has sent me to heal the brokenhearted, to preach deliverance to the captives, and recovering of sight to the blind, to set at liberty those that are bruised.

When GOD has his hands on your life you don't have to do anything. Let whoever fights, argues, debates, tweets, texts, blogs, let them try to scandalize your name.

GOD is giving you permission to do absolutely nothing. Stand back and watch and see what GOD is getting ready to do for you. You have exerted so much strength trying to defend yourself, fight for yourself, and try to speak up for yourself.

Accept people as they are but place them where they belong. You are the CEO of your life.

You can hire, fire and promote accordingly.

Sometimes you are just too unhealed to hang out. It's amazing how GOD speaks. It does not matter how loud it is around you, you can still hear him. GOD's silence is so loud you just have to be aligned.

Crying & Praying

If you can think back to a time in your life that you reflect on now and wonder, how did I manage to get through it? You would have never made it without GOD's mercy, grace and favor. It's okay to cry in silence and pray out loud or pray in silence and cry out loud.

Ask yourself this question, who saved you when you were at your lowest?

People will hate you even if they don't really know you. People's opinions of you are none of your business, and you shouldn't make it your business. You can get into a lot of trouble worrying about what someone thinks about you. When, in reality what difference does it make? The majority of people who have a negative viewpoint of you really reflect what they see and feel about themselves.

All strongholds have been broken; you have been SET FREE!!!

Acceptances

Sometimes, you just have to accept that certain things will never return to how they used to be because certain people will never go back to who they used to be in your life.

Sometimes, you just wake up and realize that what you're holding onto no longer exists.

The more you can accept what is, the less you'll be controlled by what was. You have to stop clinging to someone who has let go of you.

Stop losing yourself to someone who has already left you.

You are worthy and deserving of your own self-love.

You deserve the same love you give out. Give yourself permission to feel your own love.

Love the person you are, and also the person you are becoming.

Accept that you made it through it all-the storms, the rain, the sickness, and the pain. Stop repeating the same cycle. Break the generational curses.
You never would have made it without God.

Not Enough

You will get to a point in life where you don't have enough energy to keep letting people come into your life and do you any kind of way. You realize you don't have the strength in your life to let people come in and lead you on to make you feel like they want to be a part of your life and they know they really don't.

Everybody has flaws, but some people are dishonest about their intentions. Instead of being honest with you, they throw stone and then hide.

I understand that you are tired of being hurt, tired of people dragging you, tired of repeating the same painful cycle. But remember, the pain and disappointment has no weight if you don't sit on it.

It's extremely important to choose you even if you have to piss some people off. I feel bad for the people who didn't value you enough to commit to you.

I feel bad for the people who didn't think you weren't worth committing to too.

Because the ones who threw Shadrach, Meshach, and the Abednego into the fire were the ones who got consumed by the flames.

GOD will send you someone into your life who sees your true value and is willing to prioritize you above all others. GOD will bring someone who will never think that it's not an inconvenience to be held accountable.

GOD will only assign people in your space who can see you in your future.

Even when it hurts, no surrender, no retreat you have to always fight for yourself. Most people don't understand what that means and that's okay. There are certain things that should never be tolerated because you have got too much respect for yourself to allow all that.

Often, I think as people (women and men) we sacrifice ourselves to make things work and it definitely should not be that way, especially when it is your peace, faith, willingness to live, and worthiness.

Love Yourself

You have to choose yourself first. Choose yourself every time. Do not stay in a relationship or marriage and suffer in silence. Either you grow together or grow apart.

It happens, not everybody is meant to be together even if you feel that you are.

Choosing yourself does not make you a bad person. There is absolutely nothing wrong with being selfish with yourself and your peace.

Trust the other person will definitely choose themselves if they need to. If you don't love yourself first, you can never love anyone else.

Sometimes people will love you the way you love yourself. Not loving yourself, the person you are in a relationship or marriage with just becomes a Band-Aid to cover up what's going on with you internally.

Until you figure those things out, the most painful thing is being alone inside of yourself while being in a relationship or marriage.

We as people sometimes don't realize that there are people in our lives that come with an expiration date.

Unfortunately, having an expiration date means everyone is not meant to be in your life forever. The key is to know when it's time to cut them off.

Sometimes the person you are sleeping next to can be one of many that is against you. When GOD elevates you to your next level, you have to pay attention to those people because they will start saying "Oh you think you are better than me," or "you think you are all that now that you are doing better for yourself," or "If it wasn't for me, you would not be where you at now."

Now that is a true statement, because if it was not for them, you would not have allowed GOD to come and bless you in front of them.

Also, they would say, "Oh you have changed." No you didn't change; that person just was not ready to go where GOD is about to take you.

Tell Yourself

Tell yourself that you are doing the best you can with what I have at this moment. Even when you have a difficult day or moment, remember that this is not always true. Tomorrow will look different.

Stop trying to be everything for everybody and leaving nothing for yourself. Learn that you deserve the same love, energy, respect, and compassion that you pour into others.

Enforce boundaries. Show up for yourself more. It's okay to prioritize what you have left for yourself.

Being Alone With GOD

God says. "How are you alone when you have me?"
This is the season where isolation comes with elevation.
God has to bring you to a place where you are by yourself.

You may tell yourself that if something is not working
for you, no matter how many times you have tried to make
it work, that is God's way of telling you that He is not
going to allow you to have it because He has something
greater in store for you.

We often ask the question, "Why me?" when things go
wrong or we feel like we can't catch a break.

Have you ever just asked, "Why not me?" It may not
seem like you are strong enough to go through hardships,
but you truly are. You are built for it. I guarantee that if you
change your perspective, you will see miracles happen.

Releases

Your new life will require you to release your old ways,
whether they are habits, or your way of thinking.

Understand that your ability to conquer challenges is
limitless, but your potential to succeed is infinite
Focus only on what you can control, and give the rest to
GOD. When things in your life bring you stress, hurt, pain,
or uncertainty, release them to GOD.

"GOD, you've got this, I take my hands off of it and
release total control to you."

Know that behind the temporary dark clouds of sadness,
the sun of happiness is still shining. Make yourself proud,
because this too shall pass.

Better Version

In this season or seasons of your life, you need to breathe for yourself. You may not realize that you have been suffocating for so long, trying to accommodate other people who don't even know CPR.

Why are you allowing people to put a plastic bag over your head, choking you with their expectations, when they haven't even met their own goals in life?

You have to enter every season of life living for yourself, not for others.

God has given you permission to live for yourself. Don't allow anyone to bring you down.

Don't allow anyone to treat you as if you are an option. Be the person GOD has already designed you to be, a queen or king. Be that person for yourself. Love yourself first.

We spend so much time making sure everyone else is okay, putting our best foot forward for others. But when it's our turn to do it for ourselves, we stumble.

Sometimes people want to see you fail, but remember, you own your own crown.

Yes, it may tilt, and that's okay. Never allow anyone to fix it.

Adjust your own crown. Never remove it for anyone. Your happiness and peace are everything.

Forgiving Yourself

Forgiveness is powerful, yet very necessary. Many times we think that forgiving someone for what they did or said is sufficient, but it's not.

Once you embark on the path of healing, you will understand why it's not enough.

On your journey, you must first forgive yourself. Forgive yourself for all the times you knew better but didn't do better. Forgive yourself for allowing disrespect, betrayal, belittling to occur. **FORGIVE YOURSELF!**

After you have forgiven yourself, then and only then can you firmly close the door to past situations and move forward with your healing, holding your head high.

Surround yourself with like-minded people who genuinely wants you to be the best versions of you.

Sometimes, we fail to realize that the challenges sent by the enemy reveal what lies within us. This is why you have been facing so much. By trusting in GOD, you are making hell nervous because you are on the brink of reaching your destiny.

He understands that if you get to a place of yourself where you are in full strength, if you get to a place of full knowledge of who you really are, if you ever get over your insecurities, if you ever get over that hurt, if you ever get over that "no weapon formed against you shall prosper," and start walking into your destiny, and start to walk into

boldness like, "I Am GOD's Child," you will be
unstoppable.

You are a child of GOD. It doesn't matter what you say,
it doesn't matter what you do, and you have to live to the
fullest of your being and not die, not give up. I have always
been told you may give in, but you better not give out.
Understand that the enemy fears your confidence.

Self-love, Self-care....You are worthy! Have faith, rise
up, and position yourself for what GOD has in store for you.
Show up!

Don't lose your sanity over people who don't value you.
#

Restore

By now, you may feel like you have been through a lot in life. It is important to have faith, believe, and trust in GOD to be put back on track. You must allow GOD to restore you and get out of your own way.

If you allow GOD to restore you. He will bring you back to who you were meant to be. GOD will fix things in a way that you won't even look like what you have been through.

God will allow you to pass through the fire, but you will not smell like smoke when you come out.

He will restore you in a way that no one will believe you when you tell your story.

My prayer for whoever is reading this right now is that restoration will come into your house.

I declare restoration of your mind, heart, body and spirit. GOD, I ask that you restore everything that has been lost in this person. Amen

GOD wants you to know that despite frustration and being upset, your latter days shall be greater than your former days.

Choose Self Respect

Choose self-respect over pleasing others. Accept that every painful experience comes with a lesson. Give yourself space to grieve and courageously continue your journey.

Give yourself permission to move forward with or without someone in your life. Sometimes we may not immediately grasp the lesson, but trust that eventually you will.

Make peace with your past. Stop allowing it to dictate who you are and who you are meant to be. Stand tall in your power. Allow yourself to feel all emotions that arise, but don't dwell in them.

No matter how much it hurts, one of the most challenging things to do is to smile through the pain.

Believe in your heart that better days are coming. Remind yourself that you are rich in GOD's love, blessed, and live a life of abundance. Trust that everything will work out in your favor according to GOD's plan for you.

Tell yourself that you are incredibly favored and capable of great things. Promise to take time to observe and reflect before making decisions, as you have learned from past mistakes.

About You

In the past, I used to think that when someone tried to tell me about myself, or rewrite my story, or how I made them feel in a situation, they were painting a picture of me as a selfish , bad, or a cold-hearted person. But then I realized that wasn't it, it wasn't the case- I was simply choosing myself for once.

Stop apologizing to people for not being who they want you to be, and start apologizing to yourself for not being who you should be.

Choose to not be emotionally, mentally, and physically available for someone else's insecurities or lack of trust.

It's natural for them to feel wronged when you're no longer available, but it's important to focus on pouring into yourself and allowing others to plug into you.

The whole time, you may be suffering in silence because you won't stand up for yourself.

The Real You.

People may be unwilling to understand you now. In order for them to truly comprehend you, your heart, and your thought process, they must first understand where you came from.

Some individuals communicate solely to elicit a response and analyze your story to diagnose you.

There is a distinction between listening and active listening. Simply listening involves responding or becoming entangled in other's affairs. Active listening entails observing both verbal and non-verbal messages being conveyed, fostering mutual understanding between speaker and listener.

Everything you need will come to you at the perfect time. You can overcome any obstacle. Giving up is no longer an option!

Be grateful and proud of yourself for having the courage to take charge of your life. Let today mark the beginning of pursing your desires.

You can still be yourself while recognizing the importance of curating your inner circle and allowing only select individuals in. By understanding that not everyone deserves a seat at your table, you can remain honest and open.

Removals

Some people don't come into your life to love you; they come into your life to use you.

They don't come to add anything to your life, but to take from your life.

They don't see you as a person; they see you as an opportunity. Trust me, I have been there.

These are the type of people that don't love you for who you are; they love you for what they can take from you.

They are not loyal to you; they are only loyal to the benefits that come with you. That's why they never show up for you, no matter how many times you show up for them.

That's why they never offer help, no matter how many times you have helped them.

Stop breaking your back for people who clearly don't understand you. If the effort is not reciprocated, then that relationship has to be ended.

Points to Remember

Pain is part of growth.

Everything in life is temporary.

Worrying and complaining do not change anything.

Your scars are symbols of your strength.

Every small struggle is a step forward.

Other people's negativity is not your concern.

What's meant to be will eventually happen. The best thing you can do is keep moving forward.

Clarity from GOD

Have you ever felt like you were overreacting or imagining things? Well, I'm here to tell you that you're not. You're not overreacting, it's exactly as you think it is.

When it's from GOD, it's bring clarity, not confusion. At this stage in life, we're not going back and forth with anyone about anything for any reason.

If it was the bare minimum yesterday, it will be the same today. GOD made you in a way that you don't have to chase after things, they will come to you.

Stay on course, when the time is right, you'll know. You deserved to be loved the right way, after all the time you've been loved wrong.

Eviction

Serve an eviction notice on everything that God didn't create to be in your life.

That goes for people, mindsets, poverty, and everything that comes against the plan of GOD. I declare that you're evicted from my life. Just move forward. Trust Him and don't stop.

Stay in your own lane and own it. You can give the utmost respect but also demand respect for yourself. Understand that people don't have to give you respect, but there is no need to be confrontational, just politely vacate the premises.

Let the clown have the circus. If you argue with a clown, you become part of the circus. Accept people for who they are but place them where they belong in your life.

Winning

You are on the verge of winning in a way that will expose those who pretend to be happy for you. Your winning streak is about to make them uneasy.

If that means you open a business, whether you receive one win or promotion, when the season arrives and He continues to bless you every time you are around, it will make those who do not want you to succeed uncomfortable!#

This season, people will feel uneasy around you because you refuse to settle for mediocrity.
I declare that even if I experienced a loss last week, last month, or last year, it is still my **winning season!#**

Healing a Wound

If you understand this, then you understand it….

To heal a wound, you must refrain from touching it. Not simply apply a Band-Aid and constantly check to see if it has healed or if more ointment is needed. No, you must just stop touching it.

Because, in reality, a scab will never form over the wound and you will never develop a new layer of skin if you continue to touch it.

I don't need to explicitly state what lies between the lines because you all comprehend what I am trying to convey. In order for a wound to heal, you must cease touching it.